TRUST

Meet the World's One Savior and Lord

Kevin Johnson

DEEPER SERIES

TRUST

Meet the World's One Savior and Lord

Kevin Johnson

ZONDERVAN®

ZONDERVAN.com/
AUTHORTRACKER
follow your favorite authors

youth
specialties

**youth
specialties**

Trust: Meet the World's One Savior and Lord
Copyright 2007 by Kevin Johnson

Youth Specialties resources, 300 S. Pierce St., El Cajon, CA 92020 are published by
Zondervan, 5300 Patterson Ave. SE, Grand Rapids, MI 49530.

Library of Congress Cataloging-in-Publication Data

Johnson, Kevin (Kevin Walter)
  Trust : meet the world's one Savior and Lord / by Kevin Johnson.
      p. cm.
  ISBN-10: 0-310-27489-3 (pbk.)
  ISBN-13: 978-0-310-27489-6 (pbk.)
  1. Trust in God—Christianity. I. Title.
  BV4637.J64 2008
  248.8'3—dc22

                                                                        2007039366

Cover and interior design by SharpSeven Design

Printed in the United States of America

---

07 08 09 10 11 12 • 20 19 18 17 16 15 14 13 12 11 10 9 8 7 6 5 4 3 2 1

Contents

Start Here

It's cool that you're cracking open this book. If you've ever wanted to dig into the Bible or find out what it takes to grow in your faith, the DEEPER series is like an enormous neon finger that'll point you toward exactly what you need to know.

Trust contains 20 Bible studies that build piece by piece. You'll check out Scripture, think for yourself, and feed on insights you might not otherwise find. You'll look at heart issues that tug you away from God or draw you closer to him. And you'll get the big message—that Jesus not only rescues you from death, but he's also trustworthy as the Lord of every bit of your life.

Don't rush. Pick your own pace—from a study a day to a study a week. Actually, the slower you go, the more you'll gain. While each study is just a couple pages long, every one of them is tagged with another page of bonus material that can help you dig even deeper.

Each study opens with a mostly blank page featuring a single Bible verse that sums up the main point. These verses are worth memorizing, just as a way to grasp the awesome truths of God's Word. Then comes **START**, a brief introduction to get your brain geared up for the topic. **READ** takes you to a short Scripture passage. You can either read it here in the book or grab your own Bible and read the passage there. **THINK** helps you examine the main ideas of the passage, and **LIVE** makes it easy to apply what you learn. Finally, **WRAP** pulls everything together.

Then there's that bonus material. **MORE THOUGHTS TO MULL** tosses you a few more questions to ask yourself or others, and **MORE SCRIPTURES TO DIG** leads you to related Bible passages to give you the full scoop on a topic.

Whether you read on your own or get together with a group, *Trust* will help you take your next step in becoming wildly devoted to Jesus. If you're ready to grab hold of a heart-to-heart, all-out relationship with God, dig in!

1. WHO IS THIS GUY?

Jesus makes an entrance

John 1:29

The next day John saw Jesus coming toward him and said,

"Look, the Lamb of God, who takes away the sin of the world!"

➜ **START** If you were a star about to stroll into the party of your life, you'd probably think hard about how to maximize your entrance. Maybe you'd go with a classic drumroll and trumpet blast. Or a hip, computer-synched light show topped with flaming pyrotechnics. Whatever your choice, you'd aim for an entrance that captures your style.

If you could craft a perfect entrance to showcase the true you, what would it look like?

➜ **READ** John 1:29-34

29The next day John saw Jesus coming toward him and said, "Look, the Lamb of God, who takes away the sin of the world! 30This is the one I meant when I said, 'A man who comes after me has surpassed me because he was before me.' 31I myself did not know him, but the reason I came baptizing with water was that he might be revealed to Israel." 32Then John gave this testimony: "I saw the Spirit come down from heaven as a dove and remain on him. 33And I myself did not know him, but the one who sent me to baptize with water told me, 'The man on whom you see the Spirit come down and remain is the one who will baptize with the Holy Spirit.' 34I have seen and I testify that this is God's Chosen One."

➜ **THINK** Look at that scene as though you were one of the people present that day. You know nothing at all about how Jesus showed up on earth—like the Christmas facts about his being born in Bethlehem and tucked good-night in an animal's food bin, destined to grow up to rule the world (Luke 2:1-20). So this is the first time you've ever heard about Jesus. How does John's introduction of Jesus match up with how you'd expect the massively powerful and all-important Son of God to flash his arrival?

John the Baptizer says the whole reason he preaches is so people will recognize Jesus. What facts about Jesus do you learn from John? Shoot for at least three or four.

Trip your brain back to that scene: John is trying to make a splash for Jesus, and his carefully worded introduction all boils down to a couple of names—Jesus is the "Lamb of God" and the "Son of God." Why would those names amaze people and create enough interest that they'd pay attention to Jesus?

Calling Jesus the "Lamb of God" goes back to the Old Testament, where lambs and other animals were killed to pay the penalty for people's sins. "Son of God" means Jesus is infinitely more than a nice teacher. He's God himself come to earth as a human being. John is shouting that everyone should listen to Jesus because he's the one and only Savior and Lord of the world.

➜ **LIVE** Those are some stupendous claims about Jesus. How convinced are you that Jesus is all that?

Even if Jesus is exactly who John said he is, what would it take for you to *trust* Jesus—to rely on him for everything you need and to live every bit of your life according to his plans?

→   **WRAP**   The words of John the Baptizer contain a stunning announcement. They should also have you scratching your head and wanting more information. Trusting anyone requires knowing them well and understanding why they deserve your confidence. God designed the whole Bible—the New Testament especially—to help you figure out who Jesus is and why he's worthy of your total trust. And helping you grow in your trust in Jesus is the point of this book.

» MORE THOUGHTS TO MULL

○ What personal qualities make you feel as though you can count on someone?

○ Why are some people interested in Jesus and some aren't? How into Jesus are you?

○ Suppose Jesus had shown up in a spectacular media blitz with his name, face, and message splashed everywhere. For good or bad, how would that change your view of him?

» MORE SCRIPTURES TO DIG

○ In **Exodus 12:1-13** you can catch the background for that distinctive name "Lamb of God." That passage tells how God's Old Testament people, the Israelites, splashed the blood of a lamb on the doorjambs of their homes to protect them from God's deadly wrath while they were still living as slaves in Egypt. Jews still remember that event through an annual feast called "Passover." Jesus gives the Passover meal another meaning: He will make the ultimate sacrifice by dying on the cross. This time it's the blood of Jesus that will spare people from experiencing God's anger over sin—and Jesus' blood will also be God's unbreakable promise of forgiveness. In **Luke 22:19** Jesus instructs his followers to celebrate a meal to remember him, the event Christians call "Communion" or "the Lord's Supper."

- John the Baptizer was a wild preacher who survived in the desert by dining on honey and jumbo grasshoppers (see **Matthew 3:4**). Another unusual factoid: John and Jesus were cousins. You can read the whole family history in **Luke 1**. By the way, John the Baptizer isn't the same John who wrote the Bible passage you read at the beginning of this study. That's John the apostle—Jesus' closest friend.

- John spent his days telling people to turn away from evil or repent. He invited people to be dunked in water, or baptized, as a symbol of their coming clean from their sins. John commanded everyone from religious leaders to everyday people to get ready for the arrival of a Savior—chosen and sent by God. Even though Jesus had no wrongdoing to get rid of, he was also baptized by John. You can hear John's fiery and persuasive style in **Matthew 3:1-12**.

- After Jesus was baptized, the Holy Spirit came down from heaven as a dove and landed on him. Read the detail in **Matthew 3:16-17**. You'll also hear God the Father speak from heaven. He says about Jesus, "This is my Son, whom I love; with him I am well pleased." In that scene you spot God the Father, God the Son (Jesus), and God the Holy Spirit all at once. That's the complex three-persons, one-being entity that Christians worship as God.

2. CHECK OUT THE SAVIOR

Jesus wants you to know him up close and personal

John 1:45

Philip found Nathanael and told him, "We have found the one Moses wrote about in the Law, and about whom the prophets also wrote—Jesus of Nazareth, the son of Joseph."

➔ **START** Maybe you've been a follower of Jesus forever, with your backside parked in a church pew since you were an easy-to-tip toddler. Or maybe getting to know God feels new to you. Either way, you'd be more than a speck astounded if Jesus suddenly materialized before you and started a conversation.

What do you suppose Jesus might say to you? What would you say to him?

➔ **READ** John 1:43-51

> [43]The next day Jesus decided to leave for Galilee. Finding Philip, he said to him, "Follow me."

> [44]Philip, like Andrew and Peter, was from the town of Bethsaida. [45]Philip found Nathanael and told him, "We have found the one Moses wrote about in the Law, and about whom the prophets also wrote—Jesus of Nazareth, the son of Joseph."

> [46]"Nazareth! Can anything good come from there?" Nathanael asked.

> "Come and see," said Philip.

> [47]When Jesus saw Nathanael approaching, he said of him, "Here truly is an Israelite in whom there is no deceit."

> [48]"How do you know me?" Nathanael asked.

> Jesus answered, "I saw you while you were still under the fig tree before Philip called you."

⁴⁹Then Nathanael declared, "Rabbi, you are the Son of God; you are the king of Israel."

⁵⁰Jesus said, "You believe because I told you I saw you under the fig tree. You will see greater things than that." ⁵¹He then added, "Very truly I tell you, you will see 'heaven open, and the angels of God ascending and descending on' the Son of Man."

➜   **THINK**   Why is Philip all wound up about getting Nathanael to come and see Jesus?

"The Messiah" was the special servant of God that the Old Testament said would come to rescue the world. "The Law and the prophets" is a fast way to say "the Old Testament writings" that predicted the Savior's arrival.

Nathanael isn't immediately wowed by the invite. What does Jesus do to convince Nathanael of who Jesus is?

Does that tactic work? What does Nathanael decide about Jesus?

➔ **LIVE** Jesus displays some supernatural knowledge of Nathanael. He knows where Nate was—under a fig tree, a popular spot not just to rest, but to reflect on God. He knows who he is—a guy of pure heart and honest questions. Yet Jesus says this knowledge is just the start of the amazing things Nathanael will see.

If you had the chance to ask Jesus for one thing that would convince you he's for real, what would it be?

Picture Jesus showing up, staring you in the eyes, and saying, "I know you, and I want you to get to know me." Rate your thrill on a scale of 1 to 10 (1=total apathy, 10=total excitement). Explain.

➔ **WRAP** There's nothing better than a caring parent, pastor, or friend who prods you toward God. But you only experience a relationship with God when you see and follow Jesus for yourself. Jesus won't grab you by the scruff and shout in your face. The choice to enjoy his friendship—or not—is up to you.

»   MORE THOUGHTS TO MULL

○   Who do you know who prods you to get to know Jesus better?

○   When people try to tell you about God, would you rather have them say more or shut up? How come?

○   Talk to one or two people you know who are big into telling people about Jesus. Ask them why they do what they do. What do you think of their enthusiasm and motivation?

»   MORE SCRIPTURES TO DIG

○   That unusual phrase in verse 51, "angels of God ascending and descending on the Son of Man" echoes an Old Testament story. It's like Jesus is saying, "Hey—when I arrived the heavens split open! Now you're gonna see what God is like." You can read about it in **Genesis 28:12**.

○   Philip and Nathanael weren't the only people who bolted to follow Jesus. Check out a couple more stories in **Luke 5:1-11** and **Luke 5:27-32**.

○   The chance to check out Jesus up close and personal didn't end in the days of Philip and Nathanael. Another key passage shows that the invitation to get to know Jesus is for everyone. In **Revelation 3:20** Jesus says, "Here I am! I stand at the door and knock. If anyone hears my voice and opens the door, I will come in and eat with them, and they with me." Just like now, eating together back in Bible times was a sign of acceptance, shared values, and friendship. You can't chow down with Jesus at your most-loved food joint, but you *can* tell him you want to know him better. That's a desire he'll always fulfill.

○   You might still feel ripped off that you don't have the chance to meet Jesus in person. See what **John 20:24-31** says about that—especially verses 29-31. It's simultaneously challenging and encouraging.

3. THE BIG GULP

Jesus will quench your thirst

John 7:37

On the last and greatest day of the Festival, Jesus stood and said in a loud voice,

"Let anyone who is thirsty come to me and drink."

➜ **START** A hundred times a day, people try to point you down their brightly lit paths to the sweet life. Friends and strangers alike promise you total bliss if you score the goal, buy the stuff, join the clique, grab the guy or girl, or go wacky on weed. Each promise is a puzzle: Will that thing actually satisfy you?

Make a list: Who's tried to sell you on the idea that something will make you mildly happy—or wildly delirious? What did they suggest?

➜ **READ** John 7:37-39

> ³⁷On the last and greatest day of the Festival, Jesus stood and said in a loud voice, "Let anyone who is thirsty come to me and drink. ³⁸Whoever believes in me, as Scripture has said, rivers of living water will flow from within them." ³⁹By this he meant the Spirit, whom those who believed in him were later to receive. Up to that time the Spirit had not been given, since Jesus had not yet been glorified.

➜ **THINK** Jesus never hopped atop a lunchroom table to shout his message, but what he does here is pretty close. This scene happens on the day when a priest would draw a golden pitcher of water from a famous pool in Jerusalem, then carry it back to the temple and pour it on the altar as a gift to God. The sacred act was a symbol of how God met the needs of his people when they wandered around homeless in the parched desert. Jesus shouts to the crowds that he's offering something that beats even that.

What kind of thirst do you think Jesus is talking about?

What does Jesus promise to people who come to him to "drink"? What sounds so great about that?

That's an enormous promise. To whom does it apply?

➔ **LIVE** You weren't part of the crowd when Jesus made his big-gulp promise, but you might as well have been. After all, he invites anyone who thirsts to come to him, and he says whoever believes in him will gush living water.

With a world full of people making you all kinds of promises, do you buy Jesus' words? Why—or why not?

Think hard: What kind of satisfaction can Jesus give you that nothing else can?

How would you explain all this to friends who don't buy that Jesus offers something totally unique?

➜ **WRAP** Jesus wouldn't deny that life is full of fun and good things that fill you up for a while. (In fact, James 1:17 says those gifts come from God.) Yet Jesus claims to be enormously better than anything you might expect, exquisitely more than you dare to dream about. He doesn't offer you something. He offers you someone. He promises a relationship with himself that's so close it floods you from the insides out, with a nearness that happens through the presence of the Holy Spirit living in you. That's tough to understand, but easy to experience. It's a real promise made straight to you. (You'll catch more on the Holy Spirit in Study 10.)

» MORE THOUGHTS TO MULL

○ When do you feel close to God? When does it feel like God is far away from you?

○ When Jesus seems far away, how can you be sure he's really right there with you?

○ Here's a pointed question: If you could have anything in the world, what would you rather grab than a tight relationship with Jesus? What's the appeal?

» MORE SCRIPTURES TO DIG

○ Scope out what the apostle Paul says in **Philippians 3:7-11** about the untoppable awesomeness of knowing Jesus. Paul decides nothing can compare to the greatness of his friendship with God.

- Jesus says he's echoing something already stated in the Old Testament ("as the Scripture has said"). A bucketful of Old Testament verses tell how God's Spirit will quench your thirst. See what **Isaiah 44:1-5** says about how God will fill up you and your life. And look at the unending satisfaction offered in **Isaiah 55:1-2**, where God declares that his offer is free to you, if you want it.

- Jesus makes his I-will-quench-your-thirst claim in a few other cool spots. In **John 4:10-14** he calls himself "living water," telling an outcast woman that anyone who comes to him will never thirst again. In **John 6:35** he makes the same claim through a different metaphor. He calls himself "the bread of life" and swears he will stuff you full forever.

- **John 7:40-49** shows people's reactions to Jesus' claims. Some hear his words and conclude he is "the Christ," the Savior sent by God. Others are confused about where Jesus came from; they think he can't possibly be the Savior because they don't realize he was born in Bethlehem. (The Old Testament Scriptures say the Savior would come from Bethlehem, the hometown of the great King David.) And notice what the religious leaders think about Jesus—they want to kill him!

4. YOUR REALLY GOOD LIFE

Jesus leads you to life at its best

John 10:10

"The thief comes only to steal and kill and destroy;

I have come that they may have life, and have it to the full."

➜ **START** There's a thought that—sooner or later—scampers through most people's brains: Jesus has a hidden goal, a well-hatched plan to smash all fun and ruin life for anyone who lives by his commands. Truth is, Jesus never hides the fact that following him can get tough. But for every loss there are countless gains when you trust him to take you through life.

What are the good and bad things about being a Christian—the pros and cons? Jot down what you think:

the good *the bad*

➜ **READ** John 10:10-15

Jesus said: [10]"The thief comes only to steal and kill and destroy; I have come that they may have life, and have it to the full. [11]I am the good shepherd. The good shepherd lays down his life for the sheep. [12]The hired hand is not the shepherd and does not own the sheep. So when he sees the wolf coming, he abandons the sheep and runs away. Then the wolf attacks the flock and scatters it. [13]The man runs away because he is a hired hand and cares nothing for the sheep. [14]I am the good shepherd; I know my sheep and my sheep know me—[15]just as the Father knows me and I know the Father—and I lay down my life for the sheep."

➜ **THINK** Sheep aren't totally stupid, but they can't survive without protection and care. In Jesus' time the shepherd led his flock into a pen each night. It wasn't your standard chain-link fence designed to keep your dog in the yard. It was a stone or mud-brick structure or even a cave with a single entrance where the shepherd slept, ready to battle any enemy wielding fangs or a fork.

Jesus calls himself "the good shepherd." How does his care for the sheep differ from what anyone else does?

The second half of verse 10 is one of Jesus' most famous sayings. What does it tell you about how he wants to run your life?

What's the greatest deed Jesus is willing to do for you?

➜   **LIVE**   Who can you spot in your world who acts like a thief or treats others as a wolf treats sheep—always out to steal, kill, destroy, and devour?

God says he treats you nothing like that. So how have you seen God's kindness? What good things do you have because you belong to him?

➜ **WRAP**   It may stab your pride to admit you're sheep-like, that you need the protection and provision that come only from God. And you'll never accept that care from Jesus unless you're convinced he's really the Good Shepherd who came to give you life. So what do you think? Roll together your pros and cons of being a Christian with Jesus' claim that he came to give you life. Do you believe all this stuff? Circle what you really think, not what you think you're supposed to answer:

True   False   Yep, I'm like a sheep; I need God's protection and care.

True   False   Yep, Jesus is a good shepherd.

True   False   Yep, since I'm a sheep, I want to trust Jesus to be my shepherd.

» MORE THOUGHTS TO MULL

O   Think of three people in your life who know Jesus well. Ask them why they decided to follow Jesus. Better yet, ask them why they *keep* following Jesus.

O   Knowing that Jesus has your back sounds great, but your life is more sophisticated than a sheep's life. As you get to know more and more of the Bible, you see the big picture of what it looks like to follow Jesus. For now: What do you think Jesus does NOT promise you? Does following Jesus mean your life will always be perfect?

○ When Jesus used sheep and a shepherd as a way of describing his care for people, everyone in his day understood what he was saying because they knew all about sheep keeping. It was a major part of their lifestyles and economy. If Jesus showed up today and grabbed a modern example to explain what he's like, what might he say? Finish this: "I'm Jesus. I'm like a _____."

» MORE SCRIPTURES TO DIG

○ Look at **John 10:1-6**, the verses right before the section you read earlier. It contains cool stuff about the shepherd's voice. Note that a shepherd doesn't *drive* sheep from behind with a "Yee-haw! Git along little doggies!" He *leads* them. The sheep recognize the shepherd's voice and unique call, and they're smart enough to follow the voice of their good guy—and scatter at the voice of a stranger. Ponder: What is Jesus saying about himself? What do you suppose his voice sounds like? What makes you want to follow him?

○ **Psalm 23** gives the best picture you'll find of what it means to live with God as your shepherd. It's worth memorizing word-for-word.

○ In **John 9** Jesus debates some less-than-kindhearted religious leaders who criticized him for restoring the sight of a blind man. What Jesus proclaims in John 10 about being the Good Shepherd might not be part of the same conversation, but the contrast between Jesus and the hypocritical leaders is clear. Jesus is saying, "Hey, look. Who are you gonna listen to? Those people aren't worth entrusting your life to. Trust me."

5. GET IT TO GO

Jesus is your one way to heaven

John 14:6

Jesus answered, "I am the way and the truth and the life. No one comes to the Father except through me."

➔   **START**   You probably don't plan to hike to heaven. Then again, you probably never thought you could walk across an ocean either. But it's been done. In 1988, French adventurer Remy Bricka strapped two mini-canoes to his feet and strolled across the Atlantic Ocean—towing a catamaran survival pod containing food and space to sleep. His walk from the Canary Islands to Trinidad took 40 days.

Let's assume you want to go to heaven. How are you going to get there?

➔   **READ**   John 14:1-6

Jesus said: ¹ "Do not let your hearts be troubled. Trust in God; trust also in me. ²My Father's house has plenty of room; if that were not so, would I have told you that I am going there to prepare a place for you? ³And if I go and prepare a place for you, I will come back and take you to be with me that you also may be where I am. ⁴You know the way to the place where I am going."

⁵Thomas said to him, "Lord, we don't know where you are going, so how can we know the way?"

⁶Jesus answered, "I am the way and the truth and the life. No one comes to the Father except through me."

➔   **THINK**   Jesus shocks his closest followers with the news that he's about to leave them (John 13:1-2). Then he kneels like a servant to wash their dirty, stinking feet (13:3-11). He tells them to serve one another (13:12-17, 31-35). And he predicts Judas will sell him out, leading to Jesus' death on the cross (13:18-30), and that his friend Peter will deny even knowing him (13:36-38).

Jesus is headed to his Father's home—a.k.a. heaven. What's he going to do there?

Jesus gives Thomas some directions to get to heaven, but not the kind Tom expected. How does Jesus say his disciples will get to that snazzy home he's preparing for his followers?

Check out the words that come straight from the mouth of Jesus. Does he say there's an alternate route to get to God's home in heaven?

➜ **LIVE** Imagine yourself in the sandals of Jesus' disciples. You've been following Jesus for three years and, all of a sudden, he says he's leaving. How would you feel?

Does spending forever in heaven sound sensational—or like a complete snore? Explain your answer.

What would it mean for you to know—without any doubt—that you are God's friend? How much does it matter to you that you've got a home in heaven?

➜ **WRAP** Lots of wise religious leaders have been born, taught, and died. But the Bible teaches that in Jesus, God became a human being. Jesus did more than just hang around and teach people. He suffered death in our place and then rose from the dead. He claimed to be the world's one-and-only Savior and Lord, and he offers you a one-of-a-kind promise of an eternal home in heaven.

» MORE THOUGHTS TO MULL

- Have you ever pondered what will happen to you after you die? Assuming your last day on earth is a long way off, why think about it now?

- Even if you've always been taught that "Jesus is the only way to heaven," you need to digest for yourself what Jesus says in this passage. Suppose a friend tells you that all religions work equally well in connecting people with God. What if someone tells you there are lots of ways to get to heaven? How would you answer?

- Your goal isn't to ignite a flaming debate with every person who disagrees with the crucial Christian message that Jesus is the only one who can get us home to heaven. But who in your world needs to know what you learned today? How could you talk up this truth?

» MORE SCRIPTURES TO DIG

- Jesus doesn't fill in the details here about what heaven will be like. You need to look elsewhere in the Bible for that information. One of the best descriptions is in **Revelation 21:1-4**, where it nutshells the best points about heaven. You can keep reading in that chapter for images that attempt to tell our tiny human brains what it will look like.

- You can witness Satan's doom in **Revelation 20**. He's not exactly headed for heaven.

- Wondering where Jesus is right now? The Bible reports that 40 days after his resurrection, Jesus ascended to heaven. He was "taken up" as his followers watched, "and a cloud hid him from their sight" (**Acts 1:9-11**). But Jesus didn't jet off on a vacation. He came to earth on a mission, and the Bible says, "After he had provided purification for sins, he sat down at the right hand of the Majesty in heaven" (**Hebrews 1:3**). He's now back in the control center of the universe, forever on your side, living proof that your sins are forgiven (**1 John 2:1-2**). He's promised he'll return (**Matthew 25:31-36**). He's not just dropping by for a visit. Like he said in the passage you just read, he's coming back to get you.

- Check out **John 13** and read everything that led up to this conversation. You might guess from the chapter number on this passage that this chat happened in the middle of Jesus' life, but it took place only a few days before he went to the cross.

- Some people take the phrase "plenty of room" (**John 14:2**) to mean that when it comes to getting into heaven, it doesn't matter what you believe. But Jesus makes his point wildly clear in **verse 6**—he's the one way to God, the total source of truth, the single spring of life. He's the only way to paradise. See what **Acts 4:12** says on that point.

6. ENEMIES NO MORE

How God makes you his friend

Colossians 1:22 (NCV)

God has made you his friends again. He did this through Christ's death in the body

so that he might bring you into God's presence as people who are holy,

with no wrong, and with nothing of which God can judge you guilty.

➜ **START** Jesus not only knows the way to the Father, but he's also the one who opened the way for you to get there. The Bible says the penalty for sin is death—not just physically dying, but being separated from God (Romans 6:23). And Jesus is the one who paid God's required price for sin. 1 Timothy 2:5-6 explains, "For there is one God and one mediator between God and human beings, Christ Jesus, himself human, who gave himself as a ransom for all people."

How do you think a person becomes tight with God?

➜ **READ** Colossians 1:21-23 (NCV)

> ²¹At one time you were separated from God. You were his enemies in your minds, and the evil things you did were against God. ²²But now God has made you his friends again. He did this through Christ's death in the body so that he might bring you into God's presence as people who are holy, with no wrong, and with nothing of which God can judge you guilty. ²³This will happen if you continue strong and sure in your faith. You must not be moved away from the hope brought to you by the Good News that you heard. That same Good News has been told to everyone in the world, and I, Paul, help in preaching that Good News.

➜ **THINK** Sum up verse 21 in your own words. What are people like before they know God?

You don't have to be an ax murderer for your thoughts and behavior to miss God's totally holy standards. All of us are cut off from God. Romans 3:10-11 says, "There is no one righteous, not even one; there is no one who understands, there is no one who seeks God."

When people become God's friends through Christ's death, how does God see them?

You might have memorized the famous Bible verse John 3:16: "For God so loved the world that he gave his one and only Son, that whoever believes in him shall not perish but have eternal life." Colossians 1:21-23 is sort of an expanded way to say more about how God "gave his only Son."

➜   **LIVE**   Do you think you're God's friend? How do you know? Are you sure?

How does the Bible say you can change from being God's enemy to being God's friend?

Colossians 1:21-23 sums up in just three verses what Jesus has done for us and explains how we can straighten out our relationships with God:

> People have a *problem*—sin (verse 21).
> God has a *solution*—Jesus (verse 22).
> God requires a *response*—faith (verse 23).

In Jesus, God has the perfect solution to the problem of our sin. Belief in Jesus isn't just thinking or saying, "Yeah, I know that. I agree with that in my head." Having faith means you can say, "I trust my life to that." How are you responding to God with that kind of faith?

➜ **WRAP** Maybe you grew up understanding that Jesus died to get rid of your sins. Or maybe you've never been sure. Either way, being God's friend doesn't depend on you convincing him to let you into heaven. It's all about Jesus. When you trust Jesus—when you accept who he is and what he has done for you—you change from being God's enemy to being God's friend. God knows what's going on in your heart and head, but talking to God about it makes your faith feel solid. You can tell God something like this: "God, I know I've wronged you. I trust that Jesus died for my sins. Thank you making me your friend, and help me stick close to you."

≫   MORE THOUGHTS TO MULL

O What wrong stuff have you done—thoughts, words, actions—for which you're grateful Jesus died?

O If you're a believer, you've changed from being God's enemy to being God's friend. So what would make you want to stop being friends with him? What would persuade you to stop trusting and following Jesus?

O Tell a Christian peer how you've responded to God's solution to your problem.

O Imagine you're surrounded by people who know little about the Bible's teachings. How would you explain how to become God's friend?

» MORE SCRIPTURES TO DIG

○ Heaven is the destiny of all Christians, and you can be totally sure that's where you're headed. You became God's friend when you trusted what Jesus has done for you. **John 1:12** says, "To all who did receive him, to those who believed in his name, he gave the right to become children of God." That's not just an opportunity to become part of God's family. Because of Jesus, you have the *right* to be God's child.

○ You don't have to hold off until you get to heaven for your friendship with God to start. In fact, your eternal tight life with God begins the moment you believe, and it continues, um, without end. Check the promise Jesus makes in **John 5:24**.

○ Heaven isn't as much about a *place* as it is about a person. Sure, eternal life includes living forever; but its biggest feature is actually loving without end. See what Jesus said about all that in **John 17:3** and think hard about his words. Deep stuff.

○ Trusting in Jesus might sound too easy. But the offer for you to know God comes with no strings attached—no exceptions. Look up **Ephesians 2:8-9** for an outstanding explanation of God's free gift to you.

7. FLUNG WIDE OPEN

You can get close to God

Hebrews 10:22

Let us draw near to God with a sincere heart in full assurance of faith,

having our hearts sprinkled to cleanse us from a guilty conscience

and having our bodies washed with pure water.

➜ **START** With fists and forearms, you hammer the front door of a shimmering palace, hoping your continual pounding will convince someone inside to open the door wide. When the door stays shut, you drop to your knees and press an eyeball close to an old-school keyhole and gaze inside. While everyone else is having a ball at the party, you wonder: What's the key...that will turn this lock...open the door...and let me in?

This question might sound like the setup for a bad joke, but suppose you want to dart into God's sacred throne room? The Lord of the Universe stops and asks you, "Why should I let you in?" How would you answer?

➜ **READ** Hebrews 10:19-23

> [19]Therefore, brothers and sisters, since we have confidence to enter the Most Holy Place by the blood of Jesus, [20]by a new and living way opened for us through the curtain, that is, his body, [21]and since we have a great priest over the house of God, [22]let us draw near to God with a sincere heart in full assurance of faith, having our hearts sprinkled to cleanse us from a guilty conscience and having our bodies washed with pure water. [23]Let us hold unswervingly to the hope we profess, for he who promised is faithful.

➜ **THINK** Hebrews 10 flashes back to the Old Testament practice of sacrifice, where once a year Israel's highest-ranking priest slipped through a curtain into the ultimate place of God's presence in the temple—the "Most Holy Place." If he entered improperly, without the blood of a goat that had been killed for the people's sins, God would strike the priest dead. But Christ's death on the cross put an end to that system of sacrifices (Hebrews 10:8-11).

So why would "the blood of Jesus" allow you to enter God's presence?

That "blood of Jesus" isn't some magic potion of toenail clippings and bat's breath that forces God to accept you. It's the death Jesus died on the cross—he took the punishment you deserve.

Since Jesus' death has flung open the door to God, what kind of attitude can you have when you want to get close to God?

Sin is so serious that God doesn't tolerate evil. Period. Psalm 5:4 says, "For you are not a God who is pleased with wickedness; with you, evil people are not welcome." But when God makes you his friend, he scrubs away your sin so you stand before him knowing you're accepted. Because of Jesus, you can swap terror for boldness.

➜ **LIVE** Picture yourself locked out of heaven, banned from God's party because of your sinfulness. How would you feel?

How big a deal is it that Christ's death makes you acceptable to God? Why does it matter to you?

The death of Jesus brings you close to God when you first believe—when you become a Christian. If you've been a Christian for some time already, how does Jesus' death change how you get along with God right now?

➜ **WRAP** Jesus' death for your sins flings open the door to God—right now and for all eternity. You can run to him as your friend and kind master. You can talk to him knowing he's eager to hear your prayers. And you have his promise that you will spend eternity tight with him.

›› MORE THOUGHTS TO MULL

- Ask three people to tell you how they think they can get God to like them. What's the real way we're accepted by God?

- What keeps people from admitting to God—or even to themselves—that they've done wrong?

» MORE SCRIPTURES TO DIG

- Get the background for this passage in **Leviticus 16:4-22**. Before Jesus' arrival, people chiefly got close to God by going to the temple in Jerusalem. The temple's "Most Holy Place" was as near as anyone ever got. Only on the Day of Atonement—an annual once-per-year event—could the head priest draw so close. He sacrificed a bull for his own sins, then a goat for the sins of God's people. The blood was a staggering image of the badness of bad, a 3-D picture of the price of evil. But the real life-saving sacrifice comes in Jesus.

- **Romans 3:21-26** and **Romans 6:23** are two key passages for understanding why Christ had to die in our place. **Romans 3:23** says all of us have sinned—done wrong to God and others. **Romans 6:23** teaches that the punishment for sin is death—total, perma-nent separation from God and everything good. But forgiveness and eternal life are God's free gifts to us.

- Sinning against God isn't like dissing a friend. It's disrespecting the God of the Universe—an infinite crime with an infinite penalty. Hundreds of years before Jesus, the Bible predicted a Savior would take the punishment we deserve for the wrong we do. He would die in our place for what the Bible calls "sin," "transgression," or "iniq-uity." Learn more about what Jesus suffered on the cross in **Isaiah 53:5-6**.

- Check out **Matthew 27:51**. When Jesus died on the cross, the sky turned black and the earth shook. But another amazing thing hap-pened—the curtain that blocked the way to the Most Holy Place in the temple actually tore in two. It's a miraculous sign that by the death of Jesus, God forever ripped open a way to himself that no one can sew shut. Not then. Not now. Not ever.

8. HE GETS YOU

Jesus understands your weakness

Hebrews 4:16

Let us then approach God's throne of grace with confidence,

so that we may receive mercy and find grace to help us in our time of need.

➔ **START** When Steffi arrives home with the smell of beer and smoke on her clothes, her parents need only a sniff to know where she's been. After they tell her she's grounded, Steffi wails, "I don't drink! I don't smoke! Those are my friends! I want to be with them because they understand me!" When Steffi's parents point out that they were once her age and that they do understand, she objects, "You're old! You have no idea what I'm going through."

Who would you say best understands you? How do you know?

➔ **READ** Hebrews 4:14-16

> ¹⁴Therefore, since we have a great high priest who has ascended into heaven, Jesus the Son of God, let us hold firmly to the faith we profess. ¹⁵For we do not have a high priest who is unable to empathize with our weaknesses, but we have one who has been tempted in every way, just as we are—yet he did not sin. ¹⁶Let us then approach God's throne of grace with confidence, so that we may receive mercy and find grace to help us in our time of need.

➔ **THINK** The term "great high priest" comes from ancient times, but this passage says that what Jesus does as great high priest is a massive reason to put your trust in him. It means not only that Jesus sacrificed his life for you, but also that he now reigns in heaven.

Describe what Jesus knows about weakness—and temptation. What trouble could he have possibly faced?

You might think Jesus didn't face real temptation back in the day. But a glance at the Old Testament shows that lots of people were really into evil in those days—from child sacrifice to idol worship to incest and witchcraft. Life didn't get any prettier in the New Testament. Paul mentions sexual immorality, idolatry, stealing, greed, drunkenness, and slander (1 Corinthians 6:9-10). So Jesus lived in a world of grotesque evil. Besides that, as the Son of God he faced unique temptations that came straight from the devil (Matthew 4:1-11).

Ponder the fact that Christ had a genuine choice to make when it came to doing evil—just like you do. How shocking is that?

➜   **LIVE**   What good does it do us "hip and trendy," modern human beings to know that, like us, Jesus was tempted to do wrong?

What are the biggest temptations you face? How do you cope when you feel weak?

When life gets you in a headlock, how can you get help from God?

Mercy is God's tender grasp of your situation and his ability to unleash whatever resources are needed to take care of you. *Grace* is all about God's favor and forgiveness. Roll the two together, and it means you can ask God for whatever you need.

➜ **WRAP** Going to God wouldn't help much if he were to just roar at your problems and order you to mop up the sorry mess by your-self. The previous study showed why you can run to God, but this one shows why you want to run to him. You have access to an all-powerful God who understands you at your neediest—whether you need help with your homework or freedom from overpowering sins. No matter what you need, he's got it—and he's willing to give it to you.

» MORE THOUGHTS TO MULL

O What can you do the next time you feel tempted? Got any fresh ideas?

O Jesus isn't out to smack you upside the head when you have prob-lems. Write a few sentences about what he might say to you when you don't feel strong.

O Spend time talking to God today about your biggest headaches and struggles.

» MORE SCRIPTURES TO DIG

- When Jesus felt yanked toward doing wrong, he found two ways to get help. First, he prayed and dumped all his desires on God. When Jesus faced death on the cross, he was able to say, *Father, I don't want to go there. But I'll do what you want* (**Luke 22:42**). Second, Jesus battled temptation with the truth of God's Word. Spot how he fought back in **Matthew 4:1-11**. From what you see in that Bible passage, what does evil-fighting help look like? How does Jesus battle back?

- Think of an area where you frequently face temptation. Use a concordance, Bible study software, or topical Bible to find verses that will equip you to fight. Or tap into the wisdom of a long-time Christian.

- Do you assume the tug to do wrong is too tough to beat? The Bible promises that the temptations you face will never be so mighty that you can't win in your battle against evil. Check the promise in **1 Corinthians 10:13**, then hunt for a way out.

- Still scared that God wants to kick you when you're down and whack you when you mess up? God is not only eager to *listen*, but also to *forgive*. See what **1 John 1:8-9** says. God does want you to get honest about your sin—and he also has a way to get rid of your guilt. More on that in Study 19.

9. TALK IT UP

You can rely on Jesus

Matthew 6:9

"This, then, is how you should pray: 'Our Father in heaven, hallowed be your name...'"

→ **START** Maybe you're not exactly a guru when it comes to prayer. Or perhaps your heart throbs with passionate pleas for everything from global warming to your neighbor's dying dog. Or maybe you're just trying to grow a habit of talking to God about the happenings of life. Wherever you're at, Jesus has some straight-up and simple instructions about prayer—and even a demonstration.

What is prayer? When do you like to pray? What bugs you about prayer?

→ **READ** Matthew 6:5-13

Jesus said: [5]"And when you pray, do not be like the hypocrites, for they love to pray standing in the synagogues and on the street corners to be seen by others. Truly I tell you, they have received their reward in full. [6]But when you pray, go into your room, close the door and pray to your Father, who is unseen. Then your Father, who sees what is done in secret, will reward you. [7]And when you pray, do not keep on babbling like pagans, for they think they will be heard because of their many words. [8]Do not be like them, for your Father knows what you need before you ask him. [9]This, then, is how you should pray: 'Our Father in heaven, hallowed be your name, [10]your kingdom come, your will be done, on earth as it is in heaven. [11]Give us today our daily bread. [12]And forgive us our debts, as we also have forgiven our debtors. [13]And lead us not into temptation, but deliver us from the evil one.'"

→ **THINK** Some people think the only way to pray is long, loud, and lovely—using big words that sound super-impressive. What two or three words would you pick to describe the prayer Jesus taught?

The "Lord's Prayer" (verses 9-13) might sound a little stuffy. However, a different translation of the Bible captures Jesus' simple, straightforward tone: "Our Father in heaven, may your name be kept holy. May your Kingdom come soon. May your will be done on earth, as it is in heaven. Give us today the food we need, and forgive us our sins, as we have forgiven those who sin against us. And don't let us yield to temptation, but rescue us from the evil one" (NLT).

Exactly what kind of stuff does Jesus pray for?

Jesus' prayer packs in a lot: The phrase "hallowed be your name" reminds us that God's name should be prized. "Your kingdom come" and "your will be done" both want God's ways worked out on planet Earth. "Daily bread" asks God for the things we *need*, not all the stuff we may *want*. "Forgive us our debts" doesn't mean, "Lord, pay back the money I borrowed from my little brother's piggy bank." It's saying, "Don't hold our *moral* debts against us" (as in, "forgive us as we forgive others"). And "lead us not into temptation" requests God's help in overcoming evil.

➤ **LIVE** Pick two or three words to describe how you usually pray.

What makes prayer hard for you? What could make it easier?

Giant things...tiny concerns...Jesus says you can pray about anything. What's going on in your life right now that you want to talk about with God?

→   **WRAP**   Jesus demo'ed what the biggest quality of prayer can be: It's real. It's simple. It can be really simple.

» MORE THOUGHTS TO MULL

○ What's up when it seems as if God isn't answering some prayers?

○ Who is the best pray-er you know? Why did you pick that person? What's good or bad about imitating that person's prayers?

○ People have spotted four parts to Jesus' prayer: *praise* (applauding God), *repentance* (requesting forgiveness), *asking* (calling for daily bread and other needs), and *yielding* (telling God you want his will). Put those initials together and they spell *pray*. If your brain freezes when you want to talk to God, try using that four-part recipe.

○ Ponder these wise words: *Prayer doesn't excuse you from action.* You *should* be worried if you're praying for God to do your homework. His plan is for you to do your best and to let him take care of the rest (Proverbs 13:4). *Prayer is all about trust.* It's possible to pray for a good thing while still having an evil backup plan in mind if God doesn't show up. In that case, he won't. So check your motives (James 1:5-8). *Prayer is asking for God's best, not your whims.* Prayer isn't a magical miracle fix. You're inviting God to act in your life as he sees fit (Romans 8:28).

» MORE SCRIPTURES TO DIG

○ When Jesus said not to parade your prayers in front of others, he wasn't dictating solo prayer as the one "right way" to talk to him. Check what Jesus taught in **Matthew 18:19-20**.

○ Read the background to this amazing prayer: Jesus has been talking about what it means to be authentically spiritual, coaching people not to pump up their religion in front of people just to be seen (**Matthew 6:1-4**). Our aim is to live a real faith that, at times, happens to show up where people can see it (**Matthew 5:14**).

○ Are you wondering whether Matthew misplaced the last line of the "Lord's Prayer" that you say in church? The part that says "For yours is the kingdom and the power and the glory forever. Amen" shows up only in some later copies of Bible manuscripts. So some Bible translations show it as part of **Matthew 6:13**, while others add it as a footnote. Either way, it's still good stuff to say to God.

10. NEVER ALONE

The Spirit won't leave you lonely

John 14:16-17

"And I will ask the Father, and he will give you another advocate to help you and be with you forever—

the Spirit of truth...he lives with you and will be in you."

→ **START** Forty days after rising from the dead, Jesus vanishes from among his disciples and heads back to heaven. Acts 1:9 reports, "He was taken up before their very eyes, and a cloud hid him from their sight." If you think that sounds surprising, the things he's been talking about are even more astonishing. Jesus shares with his disciples that when he leaves, the Holy Spirit will come and jam-pack his followers with power (Acts 1:8) and his presence (Matthew 28:20). It's a promise he makes to them. It's the same promise he makes to you.

How much do you wish you could see Jesus—actually, literally, physically standing right in front of you—and have him living right next to you through every moment of your life?

→ **READ** John 14:15-18

> Jesus said: [15]"If you love me, keep my commands. [16]And I will ask the Father, and he will give you another advocate to help you and be with you forever—[17]the Spirit of truth. The world cannot accept him, because it neither sees him nor knows him. But you know him, for he lives with you and will be in you. [18]I will not leave you as orphans; I will come to you."

→ **THINK** Note that obeying God doesn't earn you his love and favor. Our obedience is a sign that we belong to him. In this passage Jesus is describing what happens in any friendship: The more you open yourself, the more you connect with the other person. If you turn your back on a friend, you'll have a hard time getting along.

Some translations use the word *Counselor* instead of *advocate* in verse 16. How long will this advocate/Counselor hang around?

Can "the world" (people who don't know God) understand this Counselor? Why or why not?

So where will that Counselor live? What will he do for people who love and follow Jesus?

Jesus is talking about the Holy Spirit here. Many other spots in the Bible fill in the details on how the Spirit impacts every person who trusts Jesus. The Spirit changes you from the inside out by teaching you (John 14:26), empowering you (Acts 1:8), giving you a special ability to serve God (1 Corinthians 12:7), and by scrubbing you clean from wrongdoing (Titus 3:5). The Spirit continues to fill you (Ephesians 5:17-20).

➜   **LIVE** As "God in a human bod," Jesus had the same limitations as anyone else, including the ability to be in only one place at a time. But the Spirit faces no such restrictions. What good does it do you to have God living "with" and "inside" you?

You have all this amazing power of God throbbing inside you. In what areas of your life would you most like the Holy Spirit to help you grow into a new-and-improved you?

➜ **WRAP** The idea that Jesus and the Father are one befuddled people back in Bible times. (In John 10:30-31, that claim made people want to kill Jesus.) So it's no surprise if these facts about the Holy Spirit are difficult for you to grasp. Yet, to make sense of all Jesus said, this is a truth you have to grab hold of: God isn't just beside you—he's *inside* you. He takes up residence in order to comfort, counsel, and change you.

» MORE THOUGHTS TO MULL

○ People in the early church struggled for a long time to get a handle on God's three-in-one nature. They ultimately called God a "Trinity." He's not three separate Gods but a "tri-unity"—three persons (Father, Son, and Holy Spirit), yet one Being (God). They're more than just separate personalities, yet so tightly united that they're still one.

○ To say that you have the Holy Spirit inside you doesn't mean you have a little bobblehead in your heart. It means the Holy Spirit resides in the core of your being—the inner part of you that thinks, feels, and decides. The apostle Paul wrote, "God's love has been poured out into our hearts through the Holy Spirit" (Romans 5:5).

○ Given all that, what about the Holy Spirit puzzles you? Who can you go to for more info about how the Spirit powers your spiritual growth?

» MORE SCRIPTURES TO DIG

O When Jesus starts talking about the Spirit, it's not a complete surprise. After all, it was the "Spirit of God" who hovered over the waters at the very beginning of the Bible in **Genesis 1:1-2**. Hundreds of years before Jesus, the prophet Joel prophesied the Spirit's coming in **Joel 2:28-29**.

O In chapters 14–16 of John's gospel, Jesus weaves talk about the Holy Spirit into his conversations with the disciples. He says it's a good thing he's leaving earth because only then will the Spirit show up (**John 16:7**). He adds that the Holy Spirit will guide people "into all the truth" (**John 16:13**). Look at **John 16:8-11** for three things the Holy Spirit will teach the world.

O You might do a double take because the Bible talks about the Spirit living in you (**1 Corinthians 6:19**), as well as Jesus living in you (**John 14:20**). It's not as confusing as it sounds. It's a sign that both Jesus and the Holy Spirit are totally God, and they both want to be completely tight with you. The upshot? Both phrases mean the same thing, which you can also spot in **Romans 8:9** and **Ephesians 3:16-17**.

O Take a peek at **Romans 8:1-17**. It gives a grand view of what the Holy Spirit wants to do in you.

11. GROWING IN A NEW DIRECTION

The fruit of the Spirit

Galatians 5:22-23

The fruit of the Spirit is love, joy, peace, patience, kindness, goodness, faithfulness, gentleness and self-control.

➔ **START**   Shooting a rocket to the moon is all about trajectory. With a well-aimed shove at blastoff, a rocket speeds along with only minor directional corrections. But without that all-important aim, it will slam back to earth or blast past its target. It's a lot like people—without the right power applied in the right direction, we wind up going where we're not supposed to go.

What do you think makes it possible for a person to choose good rather than get sucked into evil?

➔ **READ**   Galatians 5:19-26

> [19]The acts of the sinful nature are obvious: sexual immorality, impurity and debauchery; [20]idolatry and witchcraft; hatred, discord, jealousy, fits of rage, selfish ambition, dissensions, factions [21]and envy; drunkenness, orgies, and the like. I warn you, as I did before, that those who live like this will not inherit the kingdom of God. [22]But the fruit of the Spirit is love, joy, peace, patience, kindness, goodness, faithfulness, [23]gentleness and self-control. Against such things there is no law. [24]Those who belong to Christ Jesus have crucified the sinful nature with its passions and desires. [25]Since we live by the Spirit, let us keep in step with the Spirit. [26]Let us not become conceited, provoking and envying each other.

➔ **THINK**   Right before this passage, the apostle Paul said there's a war going on inside each of us. It's a fight between the Holy Spirit and our sinful nature—the natural bent each of us has to choose sin over doing right. The point isn't that any of us are guilty of all the sins Paul lists. The point is that without God's help, we all naturally head in a sinful direction.

What sorts of things do people do when their sinful natures rule?

Let's define those big words in verses 19-21: "sexual immorality" (any type of sexual relationship outside of marriage); "impurity" (moral uncleanness); "debauchery" (open disregard for what's right); "idolatry" (worshiping anything other than God); "witchcraft" (toying with or worshiping evil powers); "dissensions" and "factions" (divisions and fighting); "drunkenness" (abuse of alcohol); and "orgies" (can refer to either excessive alcohol use or sexual behavior). Notice how Paul wraps up the passage by saying, "and the like," meaning that the sinful nature can whip up lots of other kinds of evil as well.

By the way, when Paul says, "those who live like this will not inherit the kingdom of God," he isn't talking about Christians who stumble occasionally. The grammar indicates a *habit* of giving in to sin. People who consistently do those things show they haven't really received God's Spirit.

What amazingly good traits does the Spirit grow in you?

➜ **LIVE** So why call this stuff "fruit"? How does fruit happen in you? If you need a hint, flip to what Jesus says in John 15:4-5.

Think about your friendship with Jesus. How do you see your trust and obedience getting stronger and more on target? What signs say you're headed for a crash and burn?

➜   **WRAP**   Trusting Jesus means you let him take your sins to the cross. And if Jesus had to die for the wrong things you've done, it makes sense not to let those things creep back into your life. You do this by "keeping in step" with the Spirit and letting the Spirit teach you and give you new power to keep up with everything you hear. You know you're sprouting fruit when you see God changing you from the inside out, so you follow Jesus because you want to—not because you have to.

≫   MORE THOUGHTS TO MULL

O   Your goal is to head toward God in all that you do. So what's your trajectory or "flight path"? Pick one: a) I'm right on target; b) I need to do a little corrective maneuvering; c) I'm swerving far and wide; or d) I'm about to miss the moon. Another question: When you veer off course, what can you do to steer straight?

O   Make a list of all the people, hobbies, interests, and hangouts that occupy your day. Which ones help you grow good fruit? Which ones push you away from God?

O   God will always answer when you pray for him to help you grow. Talk to him and invite him to work in you through his Spirit, making you strong through his Word and training your heart to be wholly devoted to him.

» MORE SCRIPTURES TO DIG

O Right before this passage, the apostle Paul tells us Jesus has set us free from sin. We're forgiven. Totally! We're God's friends. Forever! True trust in Jesus, however, means not using God's ample forgiveness as an excuse to dive into sin. Check out everything he says in **Galatians 5:13-18**.

O Paul follows up this passage with more wise words: When you say *yes* to the Spirit and obey God, you stay in the right spot for God to grow you some more. When you give in to your sinful nature, you shrivel and die. Look up his metaphor in **Galatians 6:7-10**.

O One last bit to chew on from Paul. In the book of Romans, the apostle wrote loads of really deep words about how growth happens. Check out **Romans 6:1-14**, where Paul reminds us that when we first trusted Christ, we turned our backs on sin, "repenting" of the wrong we do. Living as a Christian means we get to enjoy the fact that we're forgiven. It also means remembering to live like the new people we are.

12. ROCK ON

Choosing to build your life on Jesus

Matthew 7:24

"Therefore everyone who hears these words of mine and puts them into practice is like a wise man who built his house on the rock."

➜ **START** You could zip through the Bible from front to back, scribbling down every "do" and "don't" you find. Your jottings would jam-pack a five-subject binder faster than your hyperactive note-taking from an overload of honors English, science, and social studies classes. Now if you truly trust Jesus, you'll take that load of Bible commands and turn it into your guidebook to life. If not? Then you'll chuck those rules like last year's homework.

Why do you think God makes rules?

➜ **READ** Matthew 7:24-27

> Jesus said: 24"Therefore everyone who hears these words of mine and puts them into practice is like a wise man who built his house on the rock. 25The rain came down, the streams rose, and the winds blew and beat against that house; yet it did not fall, because it had its foundation on the rock. 26But everyone who hears these words of mine and does not put them into practice is like a foolish man who built his house on sand. 27The rain came down, the streams rose, and the winds blew and beat against that house, and it fell with a great crash."

➜ **THINK** Explain what happens to the wise guy in Jesus' story. What does he do—and what are the results?

Sum up Jesus' point: He wants people to do what with his teaching?

These words are the punch line to Jesus' most famous collection of teach-ings—so famed that it has its own name, the "Sermon on the Mount." If you want to load up on God's guide to the good life, read what else Jesus says in Matthew 5–7. Some highlights: He starts by telling how to get truly happy (5:1-12). Then he details God's commands for standing out from the rest of the world (5:13-16), handling anger (5:21-26), righteous sex (5:27-32), dealing with enemies (5:38-48), praying with the right atti-tude (6:5-15 and 7:7-12), not stuffing yourself with stuff (6:25-34), and not judging others (7:1-5).

How is it possible to hear God's words but not put them into practice? What does that look like?

➜   **LIVE** Let's suppose you're the guy who's building on the beach and having a heap of fun—until the waves come along and knock over your sand castle. Isn't it better to have at least gotten in on some of the fun before the destruction occurred? Why—or why not?

How much trust does it take for you to obey the commands of Jesus—to put his words into practice?

What are the toughest situations you face—the ones where it's most difficult for you to do what you know is right? What could change that for you?

➜   **WRAP**   You might not be cool with all God's rules. In order to do exactly what Jesus says, you need faith in who he is and how he treats you—and that takes time to grow. But think about this: Of all the beings in the universe, only God is totally mighty, caring, and smart. He possesses total power, so he could easily force you to obey his commands. Yet he's also the ultimate in love and intelligence, so his kind character dares you to trust him. God lets *you* choose how to respond to him. He gives you the freedom to follow him—or to turn around and walk the other way.

» MORE THOUGHTS TO MULL

○   Does the unwise guy ever figure out that he's a fool?

○   Nothing God forbids is fun in the long run for all the people affected by our actions. True or false?

○   What people in your life encourage you to build on the sand—on any thought or behavior that doesn't line up with God's commands?

○ Ask a mature Christian about people they know who've ditched following Jesus as their Master. What happened? What's the lesson?

» MORE SCRIPTURES TO DIG

○ Zipping through the whole Bible to find every command of God isn't the best way to discover his plans for you. As you work through this book, jot down some of the major things God says you should do or not do. Then, beside each point, write a reason why you think he came up with that command.

○ In this same sermon, Jesus gives us another image about being wise versus being foolish. He says it's like picking between a narrow road and a wide road. It's easy to locate the broad road because it's packed with people—yet somehow there's always room for one more. Look in **Matthew 7:13-14** to see where Jesus says those wide roads will lead you.

○ When Jesus finished preaching this message, his listeners were amazed. Unlike all the religious leaders around him, he taught "with authority"—the power that comes from knowing truth firsthand. He wasn't passing along notes he'd copied from some other preacher. Read about the people's awe in **Matthew 7:28-29**.

○ Anyone with one good eyeball can see that bad gals and guys often win in this world. You might wonder if evildoers will always get away with their wickedness. People in the Bible puzzled over that one too—but only until they saw what God has planned. Dig into **Psalm 73** for a deep explanation of the fate of people who think they can get away with all sorts of evil.

13. YOUR BIGGEST TO-DO'S

God's Great Commandment

Matthew 22:37-39

"'Love the Lord your God with all your heart and with all your soul and with all your mind.'

This is the first and greatest commandment. And the second is like it: 'Love your neighbor as yourself.'"

➜ **START**   If God wanted to make your life as a Christian truly miserable, he might have laid down some key rules that were wretched to follow. As it is, Jesus said following him really boils down to just a couple of major rules that capture all the rest. And they don't sound too bad. In fact, they sound really good. More on that in a minute.

Okay, be honest. Which of God's commands do you think are dumb—so stupid that they jeopardize all the riotous fun you want to have on this planet?

➜ **READ**   Matthew 22:34-40

> ³⁴Hearing that Jesus had silenced the Sadducees, the Pharisees got together. ³⁵One of them, an expert in the law, tested him with this question: ³⁶"Teacher, which is the greatest commandment in the Law?"

> ³⁷Jesus replied: "'Love the Lord your God with all your heart and with all your soul and with all your mind.' ³⁸This is the first and greatest commandment. ³⁹And the second is like it: 'Love your neighbor as yourself.' ⁴⁰All the Law and the Prophets hang on these two commandments."

➜ **THINK**   There it is. The two major rules that sum up the rest—love God, love others. Since Jesus puts those two items at the top of your to-do list, how bad is that? Explain.

Try hard to outthink Jesus here: What good thing could you possibly do that *doesn't* fit under one of those two commands?

Why did Jesus roll those two big jobs together?

Later in the Bible, the apostle John—best friend of Jesus and author of the gospel of John—says that if you don't love the person sitting next to you, then you don't really love God. If you truly love God, then that love will always spill out onto people (1 John 4:7-8). So you can't separate your love for God from your love for people. And if you've mastered these two commandments, then you've mastered all the rest.

➜ **LIVE** How does your life look when you love God with all your heart?

And what is your life like if you care about other people as much as you care about yourself?

Name one or two things you want to change in order to put your life in line with God's major commands.

➡ **WRAP**   Jesus doesn't want to be just your Savior from sin. He wants to be the Lord of your entire life. But you won't follow him well if you don't trust him. If you're wise, you'll want to know exactly what Jesus wants you to do—and why it's worth doing. In this "Great Commandment" to love God and love others, Jesus sums up the big stuff. In the next few studies you'll look at some majorly important areas where Jesus wants to be the Lord and Master of *all* of you—your thoughts, your words, and how you get along in your world. And you'll see how he helps you track back to him whenever you veer off course.

» MORE THOUGHTS TO MULL

○ More than a few people think God's colossal goal for the universe is to blot out everyone's fun. If you know people who think like that, startle them by asking *why*. Then cause a double startle by *listening* instead of talking when they respond.

○ Jesus makes it clear what an authentic Christian looks like, but that doesn't mean every Christian gets it. To be a real Christian, some say, you have to drag your bod to church 12 times a week. Or pray intense and impressive prayers. Or worship loudly...or worship quietly with smells and bells...show off certain spiritual gifts...join the right youth group...go to a Christian school instead of a public school...or be hyper precise about the details of Christ's return or other relatively minor biblical details. Each of those things is fine—and some are downright important. But agree or disagree with this statement (and then explain why): All of those things are pointless if your faith doesn't start and end with loving God and loving others.

» MORE SCRIPTURES TO DIG

○ In this Bible passage, we spot two groups of religious leaders. The Pharisees seek to sway the crowds of ordinary people, while the Sadducees seek political power and influence among leaders. Both groups try to trick Jesus into saying something stupid because both see Jesus as a threat to their own popularity. Jesus knows these leaders are like some church folk who *look* totally religious yet miss the point about really knowing God. Jesus doesn't have much patience for people who say all the right things but don't practice what they preach. Look at **Matthew 23:1-38** to learn about the seven "woes" Jesus pronounces against them.

○ God gave us a tight definition of showing love for other people in **1 John 3:16**. Flip open your Bible and see what love can be like.

○ Jesus says that loving him means following him as Lord and obeying everything he teaches. Read it for yourself in **John 14:15**.

○ Real obedience comes from the inside out—growing out of gratitude for what Jesus has done for you. Ponder the deep message of **2 Corinthians 5:14-15**.

14. INSIDE YOUR HEAD

Your thoughts

Philippians 4:8

Finally, brothers and sisters, whatever is true, whatever is noble, whatever is right, whatever is pure, whatever is lovely, whatever is admirable— if anything is excellent or praiseworthy—think about such things.

➜ **START** Your full-grown adult cranium will contain upwards of 100 billion brain cells. Since God is the only being in the universe with flawless X-ray vision, he's the only one who knows for certain what's going on inside that brain of yours. The Bible says our thoughts can be zeroed in on God, or our heads can be a virtual sewer of anger, worry, jealousy, lust, and more. Letting Jesus rearrange your brain—putting him in charge of your thoughts so they line up with his—is a significant sign that you're making him Lord of your life. Here's a start.

➜ **READ** Philippians 4:6-8

> [6]Do not be anxious about anything, but in every situation, by prayer and petition, with thanksgiving, present your requests to God. [7]And the peace of God, which transcends all understanding, will guard your hearts and your minds in Christ Jesus. [8]Finally, brothers and sisters, whatever is true, whatever is noble, whatever is right, whatever is pure, whatever is lovely, whatever is admirable—if anything is excellent or praiseworthy—think about such things.

➜ **THINK** Life puts you in the middle of stuff that can scare you out of your shoes. What can you do with your worry?

Prayer and *petition* sound like the same thing—almost as if you're supposed to just "ask and ask!" Actually, the word for *prayer* here refers to worship—telling God he's great. *Petition* means to ask—sharing your requests with God.

God promises something will happen in your heart when you pray in this way. So what should you expect?

Slight subject change: In this passage, with what kinds of *good* stuff does God suggest you fill your brain?

True means valid, reliable, and honest. *Noble* suggests things that conform to God's standards. *Pure* refers to that which is morally clean, lovely, pleasing, or agreeable. And *admirable* means what is praiseworthy, attractive, and what rings true to the highest standards.

➜   **LIVE**   This Bible passage claims you can pray instead of puking with worry. Good idea or bad idea?

Suppose you just dumped a problem on God. How do you expect to feel? Instant peace?

God tells you to fill your head with superb thoughts, then he lays out the details. So how much of what goes on in your head doesn't even come close to that standard of thinking about what is true...noble...right...pure...lovely...admirable...excellent...and praiseworthy?

Your head's contents can be stinkin' or sweet, depending on what you allow to live in there. And brain change doesn't happen automatically. 1 Thessalonians 5:21 says you need to test truth and "hold on to what is good." You push bad stuff out by replacing it with good. With what spotless topics and interests can you fill your mind?

→ **WRAP** More than any other generation, you live in a flood of data, images, and impressions. If you don't actively filter what you let into your brain, you'll never have any room for Jesus. And what you let rule inside of you ultimately determines the person you become. Like an old proverb says, "As you think in your heart, so you are." If your head and heart follow Jesus, so will the rest of your life.

» MORE THOUGHTS TO MULL

O Quick: What were you thinking about a minute ago? Fifteen minutes ago? How about yesterday—ten minutes before the end of math class?

O Set your watch or another alarm to go off in an hour. At the sound of the beep, write down what you're thinking about. See if you spot any of these: hatred, jealousy, lust, envy, put-downs, meanness, racism, or despair. Or are you having good and happy thoughts?

- What—or who—is the biggest worry in your life right now? What can you tell God about the stuff that makes you wake up with your stomach turned inside out?

- How often does thankfulness pop to the surface of your thinking?

» MORE SCRIPTURES TO DIG

- Thinking like Jesus starts and ends with the Bible. But in between, God also teaches you loads more during your everyday life. Look at **2 Timothy 3:16-17** to see the indispensable role the Bible plays in shaping your mind.

- The passage that begins this study isn't the only Bible chunk that promises peace to those who pray. **1 Peter 5:7** says, "Cast all your anxiety on him because he cares for you." And **Isaiah 26:3-4** says, "You will keep in perfect peace those whose minds are steadfast, because they trust in you. Trust in the Lord forever, for the Lord, the Lord, is the Rock eternal."

- People do atrocious things—and their actions don't spring from out of nowhere. Evil starts on the *inside*. See how Jesus describes the root of our problems in **Matthew 15:19**.

- Read **2 Corinthians 10:2-5** to find out how you can take control of your thoughts. When the apostle Paul wrote that passage, he had in mind a certain fortress that sat on top of a hill almost 2000 feet high. It towered over the city of Corinth, the hometown of his readers. His point? God's truth can knock down even that kind of stronghold.

15. WILD WORDS

Your mouth

James 3:5

The tongue is a small part of the body, but it makes great boasts.

Consider what a great forest is set on fire by a small spark.

➜   **START**   The words that pour from your mouth are a major chunk of how you interact with people in your world—especially if you blab a lot. When God wants to change you, he starts in your head by revamping how you think. But getting your tongue under control is one of the huge things he wants to happen next. You can't claim that Jesus is Lord of your life if you don't allow him to be the Master of your mouth.

So when put-downs start flying, are you more likely to do the slamming—or to get slammed?

➜   **READ**   James 3:3-10

³When we put bits into the mouths of horses to make them obey us, we can turn the whole animal. ⁴Or take ships as an example. Although they are so large and are driven by strong winds, they are steered by a very small rudder wherever the pilot wants to go. ⁵Likewise, the tongue is a small part of the body, but it makes great boasts. Consider what a great forest is set on fire by a small spark. ⁶The tongue also is a fire, a world of evil among the parts of the body. It corrupts the whole person, sets the whole course of one's life on fire, and is itself set on fire by hell. ⁷All kinds of animals, birds, reptiles and sea creatures are being tamed and have been tamed by human beings, ⁸but no one can tame the tongue. It is a restless evil, full of deadly poison. ⁹With the tongue we praise our Lord and Father, and with it we curse human beings, who have been made in God's likeness. ¹⁰Out of the same mouth come praise and cursing. My brothers and sisters, this should not be.

➜ **THINK** What's the big point of all that imagery—horses, rudders, and sparks?

According to this passage, what's the worst effect your tongue can have? Spot at least three outcomes.

➜ **LIVE** The evils of the tongue come from hell itself, and your tongue can set life ablaze. So when have you uttered a verbal spark that ignited a forest fire?

If it's easier to clamp shut the jaws of an alligator than to control what you say, why try?

What's the best way you've come up with to keep your tongue from trashing others?

This passage hints at a solution to misbehaving mouths. The problem comes from inside, so the fix must happen within you. Jesus said it even more clearly: "The mouth speaks the things that are in the heart" (Matthew 12:34, NCV). If you want to change what comes out of your mouth, ask God to help you change what goes on in your heart.

➔ **WRAP** Just because you think an ugly thought, that doesn't mean you should let it past your lips. But taming your tongue is a monster challenge, and mastering what you say signals enormous maturity. Right before this Bible passage, James says, "We all stumble in many ways. Those who are never at fault in what they say are perfect, able to keep their whole body in check" (James 3:2). You're doing well when you stifle the tasteless words that want to pop from your mouth. But you're making even bigger progress when you start to *think* differently. Ask God to clean your heart and mind of hurtful thoughts so they don't spew out with what you say.

≫   MORE THOUGHTS TO MULL

● How many hurtful things do you say each day? Take a guess for now, and then tomorrow—actually keep track of the times you say hurtful things (and the times you're tempted to). Obviously your goal isn't to see how many brutal things you can say, but to notice how much help you need from God to put a leash on that wild thing inside your mouth. Talk to him about what you discover.

● Who else do you know who wants to work on improving what they say and how they say it? How can you keep each other on track?

○ Here's a whole nother type of mouth madness. Why would the Bible ban telling lies, as it does in Exodus 20:16 and Ephesians 4:25?

» MORE SCRIPTURES TO DIG

○ While this Bible passage from James focuses on how your mouth can blaze hot enough to char toast, check out **Ephesians 4:29** for an amazingly simple way you can know if your words are truly good.

○ Your mother isn't the only one who's concerned if you have a potty mouth. Look at **Ephesians 5:4** to learn what kinds of talk aren't fit for your mouth.

○ Jesus cut up the religious teachers of his day because they used brute force to discipline their outsides, while letting sin run wild on their insides. He said they were like freshly painted tombs—pretty on the surface, but full of dead people's bones underneath (**Matthew 23:27**). Look up **Matthew 23:25-26** for Jesus' insights regarding what your insides have to do with your outward behavior—and some wise words about where to start when you want to change.

○ Have a look at the passages that come before and after this Bible hunk on taming the tongue. In **James 1:19–2:26** there's strong teaching on living up to what you claim to believe and not playing favorites among people. In **James 3:13-18** there's a load on how wise people don't use their smarts to brutalize others. How you wield your tongue is a bridge between both points.

16. YOUR PARENTAL UNITS

Your relationships—parents

Luke 2:51-52

Then he went down to Nazareth with them and was obedient to them...

And as Jesus grew up, he increased in wisdom and in favor with God and people.

➜ **START**   This next Bible chunk might sound like it comes fresh from a whacked-out Web page—as if anyone knows what Jesus was like when he was about your age. Actually, this intriguing scrap—showing Jesus when he was 12—is straight from God's Word. You'll jump in mid-story, where you'll witness Jesus' earthly parents enjoying a panic attack. And here's why: While on a family trek to the Holy City of Jerusalem, they misplaced the world's one and only Savior and Lord. In this snippet they've just found Jesus after he's gone missing for three days. Watch how Jesus and Mary and Joseph all get along.

Before you start: What do you think Jesus was like as a junior higher?

➜ **READ**   Luke 2:46-52

> 46After three days they found him in the temple courts, sitting among the teachers, listening to them and asking them questions. 47Everyone who heard him was amazed at his understanding and his answers. 48When his parents saw him, they were astonished. His mother said to him, "Son, why have you treated us like this? Your father and I have been anxiously searching for you."
>
> 49"Why were you searching for me?" he asked. "Didn't you know I had to be in my Father's house?" 50But they did not understand what he was saying to them.
>
> 51Then he went down to Nazareth with them and was obedient to them. But his mother treasured all these things in her heart. 52And as Jesus grew up, he increased in wisdom and in favor with God and people.

➜ **THINK** It doesn't seem likely that Jesus was a nerdy little momma's boy. He was a country kid who managed to survive in the biggest city of his homeland for three days—on his own. When Jesus' parents catch up with him, what's he up to?

The religious leaders who hung out at the temple wouldn't have been wowed by the questions of most teenagers. They were accustomed to the probing logic of ancient academies, but Jesus apparently displayed unusually brilliant spiritual insight. And he does more than just ask questions. He also gives answers and spots things in Scripture that the hotshots had never heard of.

Jot down a few words to describe how Jesus responds to his parents when they show up. (How does he talk? What all does he do?)

How does Luke 2:52 sum up Jesus? Does it sound good—or not? Why?

➜ **LIVE** Jesus knew all about the Old Testament commandment to "honor your father and your mother" (Exodus 20:12). How do you "honor" your parents? And how are you feeling about that instruction?

The New Testament echoes that core command of God. It even includes the Old Testament reminder of why obedience matters: "Children, obey your parents in the Lord, for this is right. 'Honor your father and mother'—which is the first commandment with a promise—'so that it may go well with you and that you may enjoy long life on the earth'" (Ephesians 6:1-3).

What benefits do you receive when you work hard to get along with your parents?

➜ **WRAP** Jesus doesn't pounce on his parents' oversight as an opportunity to run wild. He grabs it as a chance to grow in his own relationship with his heavenly Father. In the end, the world's Master goes home and lives at peace with his parents.

» MORE THOUGHTS TO MULL

O What does obeying your parents have to do with obeying Jesus?

O Because of the way groups traveled back in Bible times, it's not difficult to picture how Jesus most likely got left behind. He's at an in-between age where his dad thinks he's traveling with the women and children, yet his mom figures he's with the men and older boys. Whoops! So when have you experienced a miscommunication with your parents?

○ Don't conclude that it's okay to ditch your parents as long as you're having deep discussions at church. What's the real lesson you want to apply from this study about getting along at home?

○ Ask your parents how long you'd be grounded if you did what Jesus did.

○ Do you think it's strange for people your age to be interested in God? As interested as Jesus was? What does it look like to be *really* interested?

» MORE SCRIPTURES TO DIG

○ Read the whole account of the family's trek to Jerusalem in **Luke 2:41-52**.

○ This is the Bible's only detailed record of Jesus when he was about your age. But see how **Hebrews 5:8** describes everything Jesus was learning as he grew up.

○ As an adult, Jesus often astonished people with his sharp insights. (See places like **Mark 6:1-5** and **Matthew 11:19**.) Even more astounding is the fact that Jesus had been wise all along. As a little kid, Jesus was already "filled with wisdom" (**Luke 2:40**).

○ Parents aren't the only authority figures you deal with in life. See what the Bible says in **Romans 13:1-6** about some others.

17. YOUR TRUE CROWD

Your relationships—friends

1 Peter 2:9

But you are a chosen people, a royal priesthood, a holy nation, God's special possession,

that you may declare the praises of him who called you out of darkness into his wonderful light.

➜ **START**   Where you wolf down lunch says loads about you—if your seat suits you, that is. Gazing around your school lunchroom, you know which group owns each spot. People sort themselves by sports, brains, musical or dramatic aptitude, clubs, favorite high, raw popularity, race, and a dozen other qualifications. You might not think your identity as a follower of Jesus has much to do with where you hang. But it has everything to do with who you are—and the people you're a part of.

Describe the group you hang with the most. What makes you tight?

➜ **READ**   1 Peter 2:9-12

> 9But you are a chosen people, a royal priesthood, a holy nation, God's special possession, that you may declare the praises of him who called you out of darkness into his wonderful light. 10Once you were not a people, but now you are the people of God; once you had not received mercy, but now you have received mercy. 11Dear friends, I urge you, as foreigners and exiles, to abstain from sinful desires, which war against your soul. 12Live such good lives among the pagans that, though they accuse you of doing wrong, they may see your good deeds and glorify God on the day he visits us.

➜ **THINK**   Whether you know it or not, as a Christian you're part of an awesomely impressive group. Look at 1 Peter 2:9-12 again and say it in your own words: Who is your crowd? What are you like? What do you do?

Verse 11 calls you a couple of not-so-nice names—because if you try hard to follow Jesus, you don't always fit in with the rest of the world. Why?

Foreigner? Exile? That's what you are, but not because you're new to your country. The Bible has this to say about some great women and men of faith: "They admitted that they were aliens and strangers on earth...They were longing for a better country—a heavenly one" (Hebrews 11:13, 16, NIV). You live in the world, but you're a citizen of heaven (see Philippians 3:20).

➜ **LIVE** In your world, how can friends get in the way of following Jesus?

And how does obeying Jesus affect the way you make human friends?

Think hard: So what sort of friends are you supposed to pick?

This Bible passage—and a horde of others—tells you to live tight with other people who love Jesus. But remember that Jesus also befriended the most vile outcasts of his day—tax collectors, prostitutes, and other "sinners" (Matthew 9:10; 21:31). Jesus managed to do right and lead people closer to his Father—all without getting sucked into doing anything wrong.

So how can you help friends meet and follow Jesus? (Remember Philip and Nathanael in John 1:43-51?)

➔   **WRAP**   God designed friendships at the center of the universe—and his plan is for you to stick tight with *both* him and the other people he made. That's real friendship—God-style. You have a chance to share with everyone around you all the greatness of having Jesus as your ultimate Friend, Savior, and Master.

»   MORE THOUGHTS TO MULL

O   Jesus didn't make it his goal to win popularity contests. But other than God, people were the most important part of Jesus' life. So how can you apply that truth in your own friendships?

O   Do Christians have to ditch and disobey God to be popular? Explain your answer.

O   Consider whether you agree or disagree with these statements: 1) Totally devoted Christians are too weird to be well liked by non-Christians. 2) Christians are outcasts. 3) A Christian who has a lot of non-Christian friends must be into some kind of evil. 4) For a Christian, popularity is a bad thing.

O What bad things can happen when you get close to non-Christians?
   Just as important: What bad things will happen if you don't?

》 MORE SCRIPTURES TO DIG

O Look at **1 Corinthians 12:12-27** for the Bible's best picture of why
   you need other followers of Jesus in your life.

O The apostle Peter is the author of the passage you read at the beginning of this study. Check what he says in **1 Peter 1:14-15** about your
   mission to stand out from the people around you. See how Jesus
   says the same thing with a couple of vivid word pictures in **Matthew 5:13-16**.

O **2 Timothy 2:22** commands you to flee evil and cling to Christian
   friends: "Run away from the evil young people like to do. Try hard
   to live right and to have faith, love, and peace, together with those
   who trust in the Lord from pure hearts" (NCV). **Matthew 28:18-20**
   commands you to go into the world and make Jesus known. How do
   you fit those two commands together?

O Look at **Acts 2:37-47** for a snapshot of friendships in the early
   church. A few Christians ultimately became a major bunch by 1)
   staying true to Jesus, and 2) bringing countless others into their
   tight circle.

18. HOT STUFF

Your relationships—guys/girls

Hebrews 13:4 (NCV)

Marriage should be honored by everyone, and husband and wife should keep their marriage pure.

God will judge as guilty those who take part in sexual sins.

→ **START**   The opposite sex: big deal—or no deal? Nose around and you'll find some peers who are obsessed with the opposite sex and others who don't seem to know another gender exists. Wherever you're at, God is your guide for getting along with guys or girls.

What does God have to do with sex—now, later, and for the rest of your life?

→ **READ**   Hebrews 13:4 (NCV)

> Marriage should be honored by everyone, and husband and wife should keep their marriage pure. God will judge as guilty those who take part in sexual sins.

→ **THINK**   Get down and dirty, starting with the final two words of that short verse. How do you define *sexual sin*?

That was a trick question! *You* don't define what's right or wrong to do with your body. *God* does. And he sets clear, unchangeable boundaries. How does God define *great sex*, the best of his plan for you and your world?

You might think God is on a rant when he says sexual intimacy is to be special to marriage. You might even think he's opposed to sex. But he's the One who designed your body to work in amazing ways. Besides that bare fact, you can't overlook the big picture of what the Bible says about sexual intimacy. There's a whole book devoted to the topic of human love—Song of Songs. While you probably won't ever choose to use this book's lavish imagery to praise the love of your life, it's a too-much-information ode to married love. Don't buy it? Then catch these candid words from Proverbs 5:18-19: "May your fountain be blessed, and may you rejoice in the wife of your youth. A loving doe, a graceful deer—may her breasts satisfy you always, may you ever be intoxicated with her love."

➔   **LIVE**   Name seven influences on how you think about sex—and how you act.

Which of those people or things drags you away from God's best for sex?

God built your body and soul with an explosive craving for human love. Your job is to manage your dreams and desires. Trusting Jesus means you actively choose to live within the boundaries he sets—that sex has one home: marriage. He expects you to respect the act of sex as your best wedding gift for your spouse. But that's only half of it. It also means staying clear of other kinds of heated sexual intimacy that God designed as a warm-up to total physical union.

Maybe this is all way more than you want to know—for now. That's fine. But you still need a plan to stay pure. When it comes to sex, what are your standards for what you watch, hear, think, say, and do?

Who will help you stick to your principles?

➜ **WRAP** It was God's plan from the start for husbands and wives to experience total physical and emotional union. So God's goal isn't to dunk all your bodily desires in ice. He wants them to heat up *when* and *where* he intended. That's God's utter best.

» MORE THOUGHTS TO MULL

O What people, places, and activities do you need to ditch today because they take you places you shouldn't go?

O What do your parents think is "too far" when it comes to physical intimacy? What does your church say? Is anyone holding you accountable to Jesus' standards—or telling you it's okay to settle for less?

O Who is your role model of sexual purity? Who can you talk to when you have blunt questions?

» MORE SCRIPTURES TO DIG

○ God's teachings about sex begin at the very start of the Bible—back in the Garden of Eden where he made Adam and Eve as a perfect match, solely for each other (**Genesis 2:18-25**). Look at his words in **Exodus 20:14**, where "You shall not commit adultery" is one of the commandments on God's "Top 10" list.

○ Don't go thinking these guidelines are too "old school" to do you any good. There's a classic passage in **1 Corinthians 6:18-20** that commands you not to sin sexually with your body. We live in a sex-soaked society where it might seem as though having premarital sex is impossible to avoid. But the people who received those words from Paul lived in a world that makes Internet pornography seem tame. Believe it or not, out-of-bounds sex was part of their religion, with ritual prostitutes helping people, um, worship. God calls all people in all times and in all places to his total purity.

○ Jesus said sexual sin isn't just a problem of the body. It starts in the mind. Check his challenging words in **Matthew 5:27-30**. Think about what you may need to chop off—and he doesn't mean actual body parts!

○ **1 Thessalonians 4:3-4** describes your chief job for now and forever: "God wants you to be holy and to stay away from sexual sins. He wants each of you to learn to control your own body in a way that is holy and honorable" (NCV).

19. MESS UP–GET UP

God forgives you when you sin

1 John 1:9

If we confess our sins, he is
faithful and just and will forgive
us our sins and purify us from
all unrighteousness.

➜   **START**   When you compare yourself to everyone around you, you might conclude that you're a pretty outstanding person. Then again, you might think you can play center in the NBA—until you stand next to a guy who's just shy of eight feet tall. Truth is, not one of us measures up to God's expectations. But God doesn't leave any of us to stew in our own sinfulness. When you trust Jesus, God starts to remake you. But you're far from immediately perfect. This side of heaven, in fact, you won't ever be totally unflawed. Here's how to deal with that.

How quickly do you admit it when you're wrong? Examples, please!

➜   **READ**   1 John 1:8-10

> [8]If we claim to be without sin, we deceive ourselves and the truth is not in us. [9]If we confess our sins, he is faithful and just and will forgive us our sins and purify us from all unrighteousness. [10]If we claim we have not sinned, we make him out to be a liar and his word is not in us.

➜   **THINK**   Suppose you just did something wrong—maybe tiny, maybe disastrous. Whatever you did to fall down, God has two options. He could shake a gargantuan finger in your face and then whack you upside the head. But he'd really like to help you get back on your feet. So what does God want you to do first?

When you do that, what does God promise to do?

Faithful means God keeps his promises, and *just* means he unfailingly does what is right. *Forgive* is about canceling the charges against you. And *purify* means God scrubs you clean of the sins that separate you from him.

➜   **LIVE**   How convinced are you that you sin? When you measure yourself by God's standards, how often do you mess up?

We sin against God and people by what we think, say, and do—and fail to do. If we're honest, we can admit that sooner or later each of us has reasons to bury our face in a pillow and bawl about our badness. Listen to this pointed translation of 1 John 1:8: "If we claim we have no sin, we are only fooling ourselves and not living in the truth" (NLT).

What do you usually do when it hits you that you've done something wrong?

What would you like to change about your future mess-ups?

So if you keep stumbling into some sin, should you give up on following Jesus?

Even the great apostle Paul admitted he didn't always do what God wanted. In Romans 7:15 he wrote, "I do not understand what I do. For what I want to do I do not do, but what I hate I do." But flip to Philippians 3:14-16 to read his vow to press on. He knew that real followers of Jesus aren't people who *never* fall down. They're the ones who get up and go on after they fall.

➜   **WRAP**   Having the guts to say you're wrong is a major way you stick close to Jesus. So is knowing how to grab hold of his forgiveness. You have two facts to keep in your head: *Fact 1:* Even as a Christian you'll sin, and sin strains your relationships with God and with people. So sin is never a good place to go. *Fact 2:* You have God's promise: If you confess what you've done wrong, God forgives and puts your friendship with him back together. Grab it and go on.

»   MORE THOUGHTS TO MULL

●   Is there any danger in knowing that God's forgiveness is always available to you? What attitude do you need to guard against?

- Part of being truly sorry for your sin is doing your best to fix what you broke. Think of something you did wrong lately: What did you do to really make it right?

- Some Christians who mess up can't accept God's forgiveness when they 'fess up. Or they confess their sins, but they can't stop messing up. If either of those descriptions fit you, find a wise, older Christian to talk to.

» MORE SCRIPTURES TO DIG

- Becoming a Christian won't make you perfect overnight. But check out the promise of **Philippians 1:6**. It says that when you become God's friend, he starts changing and growing you. And he promises he won't stop until you become like him.

- Still don't believe sin is a problem in your life? Ask your mother if you ever mess up. Quiz your friends about your ugly side. Or flip through the Bible and spot yourself in one of these lists: **Ephesians 4:25-5:4** or **Galatians 5:19-21**.

- Read **1 John 2:1-6**, where you catch the point that if you perpetually make a habit of giving in to sin, you maybe haven't understood the walloping greatness of God's kind forgiveness. Or maybe you've forgotten the fact that God wants not only to forgive you, but also to change you. If you find yourself trapped by sin over and over again, ask God to help you figure out what's going on inside you. And remember that he makes an unbreakable promise: Jesus is the sacrifice that paid for your sins.

- The Bible contains many roaring reminders of the fact that when you confess your sins to God, your sins are *gone*. Like **Psalm 103:12** says, "He has taken our sins away from us as far as the east is from the west" (NCV).

20. DO YOU TRUST ME NOW?

Counting on Jesus no matter what

Matthew 8:27

The men were amazed and asked, "What kind of man is this? Even the winds and the waves obey him!"

➔ **START** Counting from the time when Jesus called his first follow-ers to when he hung on the cross and then ascended to heaven, the early disciples had three years to watch every move the world's one-and-only Lord and Savior made. We merely glimpse Jesus long distance through time and space. They got to study Jesus up close; we meet him through a book—the Bible. But you still know enough about Jesus to have an opin-ion. So let it rip...

What's appealing about trusting your life to Jesus—and what's hard?

➔ **READ** Matthew 8:23-27

> 23Then he got into the boat and his disciples followed him. 24Sud-denly a furious storm came up on the lake, so that the waves swept over the boat. But Jesus was sleeping. 25The disciples went and woke him, saying, "Lord, save us! We're going to drown!"
>
> 26He replied, "You of little faith, why are you so afraid?" Then he got up and rebuked the winds and the waves, and it was com-pletely calm.
>
> 27The men were amazed and asked, "What kind of man is this? Even the winds and the waves obey him!"

➔ **THINK** Waves crash. Boat floods. There's only one all-powerful Being on board—and he's napping. The disciples? They're upset about their imminent doom. But answer this: Why are those guys worried?

Don't forget that many of the disciples were hard-core fishermen, so they wouldn't fret about a couple of waves. Then Jesus jabbed them with words that cry, "Don't you trust me?" Why exactly did Jesus scold them?

➜   **LIVE**   If you had almost died in that swamped boat, how tough would it be to trust Jesus? One more question: How would you have awakened Jesus—with a polite tap or a tough shove? Explain your choice.

Finish it in your own words: Trusting Jesus means...

Make a list: Which of Jesus' qualities make him trustworthy?

Maybe the biggest question comes down to this: Do you trust Jesus to float your boat—to care for you through every storm, to guide you through every moment of life, to be your ultimate Friend and Master? Why—or why not?

➔ **WRAP** You can know a lot *about* Jesus, such as how he came to earth to die and rise again as the world's Savior, or that his being God means he's Lord of the entire universe—including you. But you truly *know* Jesus firsthand when you respond to those facts with trust, counting on Jesus to wipe out your sins, feed your face, guide your life, wrap you with love, and one day take you home to heaven. Continuing to grow in trust means feeding on all the facts about Jesus that you can learn in the Bible, then putting your heart where your head is. It's choosing to live every cool or terrible minute of your life totally *with* him and *for* him because he's real.

» **MORE THOUGHTS TO MULL**

O What's going on in your life—either things happening around you or stuff inside your head—that feels too big or too difficult to entrust to Jesus?

O If you still fail to see the reasons why Jesus is so superb that you should put him in charge of your life, what would convince you to trust him? What holds you back?

O How is getting along with God like any human-to-human friendship—packed with ups and downs, thrills and boredom, happiness and pain? How is it different?

» MORE SCRIPTURES TO DIG

○ You've heard it before: The whole Bible was written so you'd know why you can rely on God. Ponder these deep words from the end of the apostle John's account of Jesus: "Jesus performed many other signs in the presence of his disciples, which are not recorded in this book. But these are written that you may believe that Jesus is the Messiah, the Son of God, and that by believing you may have life in his name" **(John 20:30-31)**.

○ If you've got your Bible open to that last passage, glance up the page to **John 20:24-29**. After Jesus rose from the dead, he appeared in a room where his disciples were meeting—even though his frightened disciples had bolted the door shut from the inside. But one guy missed out on this first encounter. Watch how Jesus responds kindly to Thomas's doubts, offers him solid evidence, and invites him to believe. Church tradition says that Thomas later took the great news about Jesus as far away as India.

○ Getting walloped by ugly circumstances can make anyone question whether or not Jesus can be trusted. Check **James 1:2-6** for instructions on how to weather the storms.

○ Looking for a model of real trust in God? Thumb through **Hebrews 11** for the Bible's best examples of people putting their faith in God—no matter what. Then don't miss **Hebrews 11:1, 6** for a tight definition of *faith*—and why it matters.

Many people think teenagers aren't capable of much. But Zach Hunter is proving those people wrong. He's only fifteen, but he's working to end slavery in the world—and he's making changes that affect millions of people. Find out how Zach is making a difference and how you can make changes in the things that you see wrong with our world.

Be the Change
Your Guide to Freeing Slaves and Changing the World
Zach Hunter
RETAIL $9.99
ISBN 0-310-27756-6

Visit www.invertbooks.com or your local bookstore.

If you've ever wondered if God is really there and listening, if you're good enough, or what's so great about heaven, you're not alone. We all have had personal questions, but the answers are often harder to come by. In this book, you'll discover how to navigate your big questions, and what the answers mean for your life and faith.

Living with Questions
Dale Fincher
RETAIL $9.99
ISBN 0-310-27664-0